an introduction to service design

how to
have your cake
and eat it too

an introduction to service design

B/SPUBLISHERS

Written by:	J. Margus Klaar
Edited by:	Markko Karu
	Kaarel Mikkin
	Dan Mikkin
Proofreading:	Lewis McGuffie
	Bethany Edstrom
Art Direction:	Dan Mikkin
Layout:	Joonas Rumvolt
	Slava Devjatkin
Illustrations:	Lewis McGuffie
Typefaces:	Speak, Goudy Oldstyle

BIS Publishers
Building Het Sieraad
Postjesweg 1
1057 DT Amsterdam
The Netherlands
T +31 (0)20 515 02 30
F +31 (0)20 515 02 39
bis@bispublishers.nl
www.bispublishers.nl

ISBN 978 90 6369 381 7

Every reasonable attempt has been made to identify
owners of copyright. Any errors or omissions brought to the
publisher's attention will be corrected in subsequent editions.

www.thebrandmanual.com

Ninety percent of North American firms view customer experience as important or critical to 2010 plans.

Eighty percent of firms would like to use customer experience as a form of differentiation.

Forrester's: The State of Customer Experience 2010

Eighty-five percent of business leaders agree that traditional differentiators alone are no longer a sustainable business strategy.

Shaw & Ivens

Seventy-one percent of business leaders believe that customer experience is the next corporate battleground.

Shaw & Ivens

Why is it
called design
21

Operations and
aspirations
27

From goods
to services
19

Form following
function
24

The first rule of
service design
26

What is
service design?
15

Personas
38

Need is never
a thing
31

Going to
the show
33

Customer
journey
29

It's an omni-
channel world
41

Commonalities and
differences
40

Why? Why? Wh
Why? Why?
11

Empathy
maps
38

How do they feel?
41

Visualisation and
non-linear information
42

The difference between
quantitative and
qualitative data
49

Talking
to people
45

Validating
hypotheses
45

Observation
56

Conversations
51

Data mining
based on insight
54

Contents map

Introduction

Why?

Things should work the way people expect them to work. If things don't work that way, then they should come with instructions that are clear, logical and intuitive so users don't resent having to learn a new way to do things. If a door is locked, there should be a sign directing you to an open door.

But things often don't work the way people expect them to work. We are continually asked to learn new ways to do things. Much of the time, we don't complain. We just grin and bear it. And if we have to use something, we get used to it until a clear alternative appears and then we switch so fast that often the company we used to patronize goes bankrupt: Kodak, Post Office, Blockbuster, Nokia, etc.

To improve how products work and how services are delivered, we must question why so many products don't work as well as we would like. We should be asking "why" instead of "how." There are so many unnecessary rules, inefficient ways of working, senselessly complicated interfaces, and bureaucratic organizations. If all products and procedures worked the way they are intended, many governments might save as much as one yearly budget every 10 years. Today, government requires so much duplication of effort, pointless work, and making people run around that sometimes it's a wonder anything works at all.

Recently a tax official photocopied my passport, in order to send a hard copy of the information to the regional tax office where the paperwork is organized. This being the 21st century and the biometric passport in question being from the same country as the tax office, I expected that they could just read and confirm the data on the passport electronically and flag the information in the database, to link with my tax profile. Why are they copying paper?

Or why can't children under the age of 18, in some countries, have access to an internet bank account, while in other countries they can? Why are movie ratings still in force when every movie can be seen online or bought on DVD without any age checks whatsoever?

There are a lot of questions being raised in today's fast-changing societies. The role of education is a good example. Most schools teach many skills that parents and grandparents believe to be important but which may be outmoded or outdated later in the child's life.

But even more importantly, a lot of information given on an everyday level is based on presumptions that have never been challenged. In some metro systems, exits are indicated by the name of the street they lead to, not by the major points of interest next to which they emerge. However, it seems reasonable that people go to places, not addresses. Contextual destination signs would make navigating easier.

When experiencing bad service or a bad product, ask yourself 'Why?" Sometimes the answer can be cost – for example, a nice charger for a portable device may cost as much as the device itself, so a cheaper charger is provided instead for the sake of economy. Other times the answer may be that the product's developers lacked foresight and created more problems than they solved. In addition, language barriers can cause confusion when the person tasked with checking a translation has weak native linguistic skills.

how to have your cake and eat it too

However, asking "why" at the right time in the development process can lead to startlingly obvious product innovations. When every computer still had a mouse attached by a cable, the cable had to be attached to the PC; therefore, this cable had to be very long. You had to crawl under the table to connect the device. Customers became used to this inconvenience until Apple attached the mouse to the keyboard, which made the cable short and sweet, and people no longer had to crawl under tables to make their equipment work.

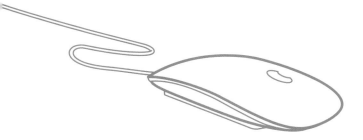

Why? Why?
Why? Why?

Ask "why" enough times, and you'll get to the heart of the matter. You may even find yourself in uncharted territory on the way to innovation and better service delivery. Asking "why" can upset business models. For example, many construction companies have stopped buying equipment and started renting it instead. Construction companies only use the equipment; the responsibility of making sure the equipment works lies with another organization. The result is tools that are in use continuously instead of occasionally, while maintenance of the tools is a permanent job which ensures they work better and longer. Why own tools and use them rarely if you can just rent when you need them?

Outsourcing customer service was an attempt to save money. It turned out, however, that cheaper service is not better service. Customer satisfaction is negatively affected when call centers are located in the middle of nowhere. Unfortunately, customer feedback is often not viewed as valuable insight but as a necessary nuisance to be handled as economically as possible.

So as you read through this book, think about your own business and why you do things the way you do. There may be room for improvement.

What is service design?

Service design organizes business from the customer's point of view. The goal is to deliver a positive customer experience at all points of interaction between a company and a customer. Some organizations have been good at this for centuries; others stink and are successful only because they have a monopoly or because the alternatives are not convenient for customers.

Some may be reluctant to see service design as a discipline in itself, when many companies and individuals have been practicing it intuitively for years. The fact is that times have changed. While delivering a good customer experience was desirable ten, twenty, and thirty years ago, it was not the only means of achieving a competitive advantage. Back then, a company could also excel at marketing or simply have a better product or high barriers to entry. Today, however, quality is universal. Any car you buy is likely to work without major problems. Most airlines will take you from point A to point B. Computers work. The difference is no longer in what companies do. The competitive advantage comes from how they do it.

This new situation has come about by a combination of technological democratization and globalization. Round the clock low cost access to the internet has created new industries (like apps and mobile services). It has allowed people to organize (from demonstrators to parental groups) and made peer reviews, outside the control of marketers, the most trusted source of information about products and services. Thanks to, and because of this, globalization and the reduction of trade barriers have made competition much more intense. People are empowered to choose what is best for them from anywhere in the world.

In this environment, the keys to a competitive advantage are the way the product or service is delivered, the way it is experienced, and the design of the product or service.

It is also important to recognize that for most products and services the purchase moment makes up the smallest and perhaps least significant part of the customer experience. Buying a new phone is not about owning a phone; it is about having a digital service delivered. Similarly, a car should no longer be a machine with which to drive but a vehicle that is connected to maps and traffic reports, helping the driver get from A to B with minimal wasted time. This makes up the customer experience, and the details of this ownership experience are what is shared online in product review forums.

This book is about improving these experiences – about designing a whole service, from the moment the customer starts thinking about the possible purchase until the end of the life cycle of the product. Improving on all the points of interaction will improve customer satisfaction. From a marketing perspective, nothing sells as well as satisfied customers. For this reason, applying service design can help you cut your marketing budget in half. Or, in other words, let you have your cake and eat it too.

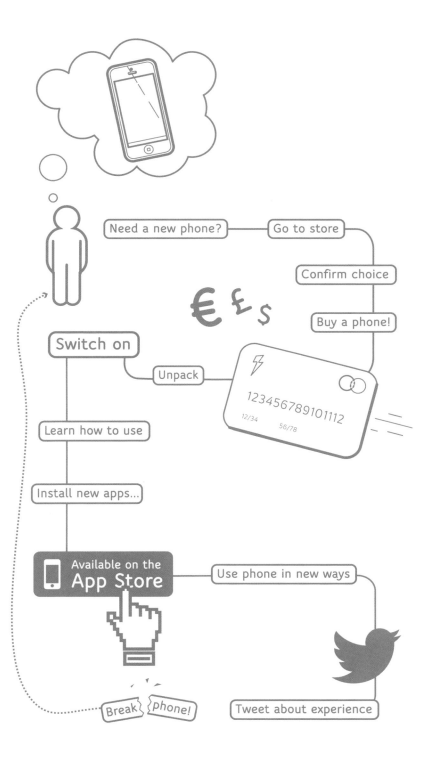

Providing information > managing expectations

A good customer experience comes down to managing expectations. If you, as a customer, know that you'll have to wait two hours for a service, those two hours become the default against which a good and bad service experience is judged. If the service is delivered in 1 hour and 45 minutes, you'll be pleased. If it takes 2 hours and 10 minutes, you will be frustrated. But if you're promised a service in 15 minutes and it still takes an hour, you will complain of terrible service – even though the net result is BETTER than the 2 hour waiting time.

Managing expectations means providing relevant and reliable information at every step of the customer service process. Many software companies are already doing a good job of providing relevant information. Great software works step by step in such a common-sense fashion that each step contains instructions for the next step, so that everyone can use it.

Signage in the cityscape works the same way. Signs pointing in the right direction must be placed at all points where there are more than one option to choose from. Furthermore, on long stretches of road or highway, signs must be placed periodically to reinforce our knowledge that we made the right decision. Anything less, and we lose confidence that we are going the right way.

From goods to services

From the beginning of the Industrial Revolution until the end of the 20th century, we have lived in a world where things were made and then delivered. Products were complicated, often unreliable, and the difference in quality and usability among similar products was clear. The cost of items was related to how well they worked. Improvements to products were made in-house, tested in-house, packaged, and then marketed. Customer feedback was gained at the last step in the process: in the store.

This industrial, or goods-dominated, logic, has prevailed to this day, but is less and less viable as the difference in quality between products disappears. As many products now do the same thing with comparable quality, the defining moment is no longer in what products do, but how they do it. The "how" is the value it delivers to the customer, because the "what" has become a hygiene factor.

A fundamental difference between goods and services is that a service is created in cooperation between the delivering party and the receiving party. It cannot be pre-packaged and delivered. It is unique every time, and different people may experience the same service in radically different ways. The gym is a perfect example: for the person in good shape who has been to gyms before and is comfortable in an environment where everyone looks at one another, the experience is largely positive. For someone determined to improve his or her physi-

cal self for the first time, a largely male, testosterone-filled environment can be uncomfortable and intimidating.

Therefore, designing a safe gym for weightlifting is very much like the goods-dominated method of the past. It can be logistically designed and stocked with the best machines and free weights and, as a result, be the perfect gym for the experienced customer. But the value received depends on the perspective of the customer, not the gym owner. For many customers, the machines look like torture devices and the free weights are intimidating, because picking the lightest one makes the user look like a wimp and the heavier ones are too heavy. Therefore, "how" becomes more important than "what."

> Designing the gym from a different customer group's point of view can change the way the gym is set up

Designing the gym from a different customer group's point of view can change the way the gym is set up – which machines and weights are included and how the rooms are arranged. This change in perspective could make all the difference, as today the number of unfit people greatly outnumber the fit.

how to have your cake and eat it too

Why is this process called design?

The design process, whether of services or products, is what gives service design its name. Design is not just an aesthetic exercise. To design means to "give form," to something, to model ideas into something that can be experienced. Design is a problem-solving discipline that seeks to address four main issues:

- Understandability
- Usability
- Distinction
- Aesthetics

Understandability

We all know how a hammer works. The form follows the function of the tool, and when we need to drive nails, we all know how to use it. A tax form, on the other hand, may not be as clear.

Why is this?

Asking "why?" instead of "what?" is one of the qualities of a good designer. Tax forms are not designed to be easy and intuitive. Instead, they are made to be legally binding, often written in legalese. They are laid out logically based on how the information will be used in the tax office, perhaps with a view to how the information will be analyzed in the computer. They are not designed from the customer's point of view, let alone written in a language most of us use on a day-to-day basis. Tax forms are difficult to read, difficult to understand. Although most of us are happy only having to go through this ordeal once a year, we are often in a position in which we have to learn this process again each year: how the process works and what it is we have to do. Imagine if the tax form were written without legal jargon, using words that people use every day.

Simplifying legal jargon. Alan Siegel at TED.
http://tinyurl.com/m548pmc

Usability

It is surprising how often products and services don't meet basic usability criteria. Those who create and sell these products and services may describe them as "designed" when in fact they are anything but. Door knobs are an excellent case in point. In North America, most domestic doors have knobs instead of handles. These knobs are easy and simple enough for adults to use, but they are difficult for children. And, today, with an increasing elderly population, doorknobs are also a challenge for those whose grip is no longer strong.

Often, products come with instructions that offset any usability shortcomings. However, making instructions available does not automatically make a product usable. Being informed about a road block without information about alternate routes is not helpful.

Distinction

Distinct means recognizable. Different from others. Memorable, if you like. Why do something, if your customers can't remember who your company is or where they got your product from? And no, this is not as unique a situation as it should be. Most hotels are so indistinguishable that it isn't possible to remember which one is which. A lot of restaurants just serve sustenance instead of unique and memorable meals.

Many businesses boast of favorable prices or excellent service. This doesn't make them distinct, however, as their competitors make similar claims, and measurable qualities are easy to copy. On the other hand, a funny guy at the counter or the coziest chairs a customer has ever experienced can have a lasting impact. They allow customers to tell a story about their visit, and consequently the business is remembered.

Aesthetics

Beauty, they say, is in the eye of the beholder. Furthermore, in business beauty is often considered a frivolous quality, an unnecessary expense, and an indulgence completely irrelevant to most customers. Nothing could be further from the truth.

As people, we are attracted to attractive people. Similarly, pleasing shapes and balanced colors help us to feel comfortable and happy. And, more often than not, a product known for its pleasing shape also functions well because a well-designed product is first and foremost a usable product. A round pipe is the strongest vessel for containing liquid. Even the simple act of reading benefits from good design; if text is readable and easy to follow, we can assume that the typeface is suitable for the task it is performing.

Form following function

Consider the humble potato peeler and the not-so-humble citrus press. In a casual survey, most people will call the citrus press "designed" but are likely to overlook the potato peeler.

However, while the citrus press is definitely visually striking, it doesn't work very well. It is not space-efficient. Although it is material-efficient, because it is cast, its package is not material-efficient. Its value is mainly aesthetic.

The potato peeler, on the other hand, is thoroughly designed. It is material-efficient, contains a minimum amount of parts, can be used either by left- or right-handed people, and has remained unchanged for decades.

One could, in fact, argue that the potato peeler is a much more fully designed item than the citrus press. Whereas the citrus press looks good, the potato peeler is designed from both a usage and manufacturing point of view to be as efficient as possible.

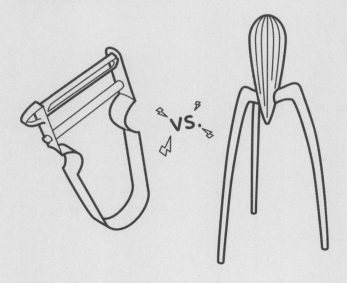

What is in this book

This book will help you understand how to find out what your customers actually value in your product or service. It will help you find out what you have to improve in order to deliver a positive customer experience.

The methods used to find out what customers value and where the real problems lie are universal. These can be applied in small businesses as well as conglomerates. However, the process of improving is unique and will always be dependent on the organization and its culture. The time this process takes is similarly related to the company's size and complexity and can vary wildly between businesses. There are few universal truths about services. In most cases, the biggest improvements come from knowing specifics about your business. There are always hidden answers that appear once you begin to ask the right questions.

Imagine that your grandmother always cut her steak in half before she cooked it, and when you learned to cook you did the same. Is there a reason to cut your steak into two pieces? Your grandmother did just because she had a small oven, not because it made the meat better. Human behavior will always be shaped by thought models, and it is difficult to change behavior before you understand the initial reasoning behind it. To change behavior, you must understand "why" things are like they are.

To answer why, follow these steps:

- Customer journey mapping
- Validating assumptions
- Touchpoint mapping
- Touchpoint matrix and improvement hierarchy

Improving and solving problem areas will come later; first, you need to find out what these problem areas are. How you do it will depend on the unique nature of your business. Design is an iterative process and the cycle of doing, evaluating, and improving may need to be repeated several times before it is finished.

The first rule of service design

There is only one rule in service design: this discipline is user centered and involves everyone that matters, such as the customer, the service provider and other stakeholder(s).

The process of identifying and solving is based on what actual people do in actual situations, and not on an imagined or idealized idea of how clients and staff will react based on perceived patterns of behavior.

The fundamental difference between a start-up and an established business is how fast start-ups iterate their service and how long it takes a conglomerate to do so. Service design is similar to a start-up. Its goal is always to make small improvements, release them to the customer, gather feedback, and improve again. The smaller the steps, the faster the results become apparent. A minor investment in service improvement always earns a return. That's more than can be said for many larger initiatives.

But keep in mind that you need to let real customers give real feedback. Without customer involvement and feedback, any improvements made may be imaginary and related to perceived service delivery, not actual value received by the customer.

how to have your cake and eat it too

Operations and aspirations

Service design is not an ideology. The goal is not to satisfy the customer's whims at any cost. In fact, service design is profit motivated, clearly business-focused and based on a proven track record. If customers get what they want in a manner that seems reasonable to them, they'll be willing pay a fair price, come back, and recommend the product or service to their friends.

That same principle applies within organizations as well. If staff works in a manner that seems reasonable to them, they'll put in effort and remain motivated and loyal. However, if the aim of management becomes control instead of empowerment, staff will feel that they are following stupid rules.

The principles of service design, can be equally applied to staff empowerment. The principles of service design suggest that a business should be organized like a backwards pyramid: customers first, then staff, then middle management and finally top management. The logic is quite simple – motivated and empowered staff work hard to deliver a superior product and/or service to the customer, often above and beyond what is asked of them in their contract.

Service design is profit-motivated and clearly business-focused!

The key to service design is to see the world from the customer's perspective – not to change his or her behavior, but to change your company's behavior.

In order to find what a small child has hidden, it is best to view the world from the child's viewpoint. Sit on the floor. What is the most inaccessible point you can reach?

The customer journey

Need is never a "thing"

People don't need to own a carton of milk. They may need the calcium, but what they want is pancakes, hot chocolate or a café latte. Therefore, as they enter the store to buy milk, their journey from need to satisfaction is already halfway complete. For the merchant, the customer just entered the premises. It is in this difference of perception that service design comes into play.

Looking at a store's sales statistics to analyze what people are buying can be misleading. The question that should be asked is why customers are buying a particular product. It is the motivation behind the transaction that determines what is bought. Anyone doubting this statement should try selling cigarettes to a non-smoker.

What do you know about your customers? Most companies know what customers say about a product or service because they ask for feedback. Some companies know what people actually do, as they monitor customer behavior. To a service design professional, the most valuable information to collect is what people do with what they bought – that is, knowing how their need is satisfied by a product or service. This describes the motivation behind the transaction.

Walking in the customer's shoes

The first step to improving the customer experience is to experience the experience. In other words, to understand what your customers are going through, you must look at the world through their eyes. The customer journey for different products and services differs case by case. However, in general this experience starts well before the person arrives to buy something and ends only after the product has been discarded or the service is used.

MIT Agelab. AGNES – Age Gain Now Empathy System.
http://tinyurl.com/8a5n93x

Try to imagine not knowing everything there is to know about your product or service. An airline pilot may be an expert on airports and planes but may have never experienced typical customer frustrations: a long queue in check-in, security, overweight luggage, crying babies, narrow seats, and bad food. A pilot's advice on improving airline service, therefore, may prove to be worthless.

how to have your cake and eat it too

Going to the show

Consider a trip to the movies. The journey to the cinema starts with getting interested in one film or another. This interest might be sparked by a poster on a billboard or a TV commercial or a video going viral and ending up in your Facebook feed. Whichever way it happens, somehow you have been made aware of a movie, and you want to see it.

Once you've figured out which movie you want to see, you'll need to find somewhere to see it. In the likelihood that you know which movie theatre you'd prefer to visit, you go online to check the cinema's website and choose a day and time to see the film. Buying the ticket online allows you to pick your own seat. With a sophisticated booking system you'll receive a digital ticket on your smartphone. With an older system you'll print out the ticket at the cinema from a self-service kiosk. And before that you'll drive to the movie theater and spend several minutes looking for a parking spot nearby.

Once you've stood in line for sodas and popcorn, you'll proceed to the movie theater, perhaps via the over-used and under-cleaned toilet. And because it's cold outside you're over-heating in your winter jacket, which you can't hang anywhere. Once you enter the movie hall, you'll discover that there is nowhere to place your jacket there either, which means that you'll spend the next two hours sitting on it.

The film lives up to every one of your wildest cinematic fantasies. You're happy. But as the credits roll, you realize you need to use the toilet again, thanks to the gargantuan soda you've just consumed. Depending on the cinema and time of day, you might instead be shown straight out of the theatre into the alleyway, because everything else in the

Customer Journey [DETAIL]
From the customers perspective

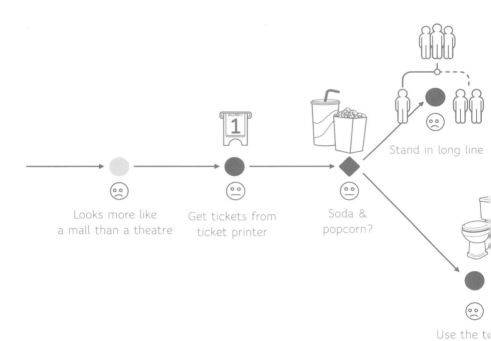

Stand in long line

Looks more like
a mall than a theatre

Get tickets from
ticket printer

Soda &
popcorn?

Use the t
It's mes

 Customer   Touchpoint   Missing   Happy

 Cinema   Decision   Broken   Neutral

 Third party   Action   Disappointed

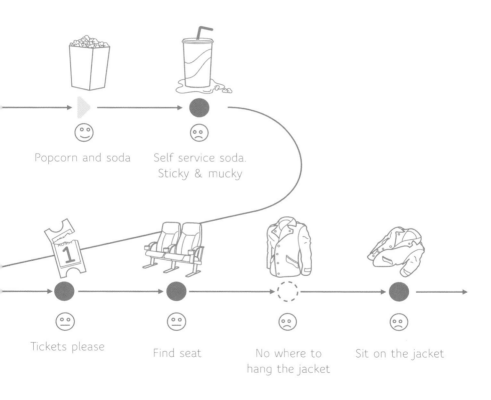

Popcorn and soda

Self service soda.
Sticky & mucky

Tickets please

Find seat

No where to
hang the jacket

Sit on the jacket

complex is already closed. And now you're standing outside in the dark looking for somewhere to pee and wondering where you left the car. The city, after all, looked completely different in daylight.

After a stroll around a dimly lit car park, you recognize your license plate and drive home. The next day (or the same evening), you may comment on the movie on Facebook or Twitter or talk to your coworkers about it, remarking both on the film and on the cinema. This in turn influences others as to whether they should see the same movie at the same cinema – and possibly even whether they should buy such a large soda.

What part of the journey didn't we like?

Toilets were the problem, both before and after. Where to put your winter coat was also a problem. Online payment systems can as well cause problems, depending on how user-centered they are.

Note that improving the overall movie experience has very little to do with creating better movies. Often, it is the rest of the experience where customers come across problems or concerns, which, from the service design perspective, could easily be improved.

Each customer group has a different point of view and will likely report different problems.

This quick intellectual exercise on the larger experience of going to a movie illustrates the essence of the customer journey. By viewing the whole process from need to satisfied customers, we can determine bottlenecks and opportunities that otherwise we might not see. The next step is to draw out this same journey for different customer groups. Broadly speaking, in the case of movies we have:

- adult couples
- kids (boys)
- kids (girls)
- families
- mothers with babies
- pensioners
- teenage couples
- young group of men
- young group of women
- young group
- any of the above, but non-native language speakers
- any of the above, but with disabilities

A general sketch of the journey can be created based on the above stereotypical description or in much more detail based on personas of real people. Personas are detailed descriptions of people that include personality traits rated from desirable to undesirable – habits, desires, tastes, media preferences, means of income, etc. In other words, a persona is a colorful painting of a real "flesh and blood" person.

Personas

Developing personas is not difficult. However, it's important to develop personas based on realistic character traits, including regular problems that real people have. A persona is a fictional character with a purpose. Usually personas are based on qualities you can easily observe, but the preferences and abilities of each persona should be different from those of the business owner or the service design professional (and, ideally, more like those of an actual customer). The goal is to create a persona that one can attach a name and picture to and perceive as believable. Perfect imaginary friends don't help. Flaws, wrinkles, and muffin tops do. Anchoring the personas in statistics, including socio-demographic and income indicators, helps keep them realistic.

Empathy maps

Personas should reflect real people. In order to understand how these particular personas view the world – and, of course, the product or service under scrutiny – it helps to see the world through their eyes. Empathy maps are an effective method of hearing, seeing, thinking and feeling as customers do. As a part of the empathy map, we'll understand what "pain" the persona will have to go through for the "gain" of the service or product.

Empathy maps study customers and collect their views of the observable competition (i.e. what customers see), the peer pressure and general opinions they encounter (what they hear), decision points and articulated needs in the process of selecting a product (what they think,) and behavior (what they do). Pain and gain reflect the obstacles and motivation of the customer.

Keep in mind, that "pain" can refer to anything from time spent in line to the indignity of having to answer seemingly irrelevant questions from a loan officer.

how to have your cake and eat it too

EMPAHTHY MAP

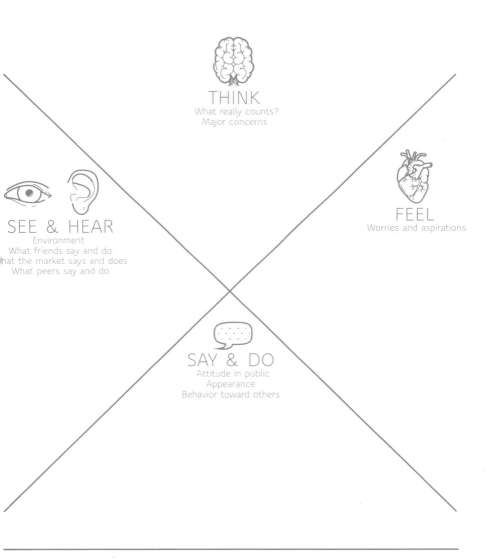

THINK
What really counts?
Major concerns

FEEL
Worries and aspirations

SEE & HEAR
Environment
What friends say and do
What the market says and does
What peers say and do

SAY & DO
Attitude in public
Appearance
Behavior toward others

PAIN
Fears
Frustrations
Obstacles

GAIN
Wants/Needs
Measures of success

The goal of the empathy map exercise is to visualize the process of decision making that customers actually experience. This process can help companies to recognize the moment(s) when customers are experiencing difficulties that may, if left unmanaged, result in customers walking away.

Commonalities and differences

With detailed personas and information from empathy maps, we can draw accurate customer journeys that highlight both commonalities of the service for all customer groups as well as the specific problems or needs that apply to only one or a few customers. Commonalities are things that are the same for all customers regardless of sex, income, time availability, preferences, etc. At McDonald's, for example, these common factors include the fact that no matter who a person is and how he or she gets there, he or she still visits the restaurant to buy food or drink.

> What is the impulse that brings customers to your business?

Potential differences, on the other hand, include a) preference of food, b) a decision to eat in, take food to go, or use the drive-thru, c) payment via cash or card, d) custom requests (e.g. no pickles), and so on.

But what is the impulse that brings customers to your business? Do they seek convenience or low prices, or does peer pressure or personal preference drive them? Is the trip to the restaurant planned, or is it a spur-of-the-moment decision? Is the trip in response to a special offer or event occurring in the vicinity? Understanding the routes customers take to your business as well as the channels through which different customer groups learn about your company will allow your business to manage the customer experience more effectively.

It's an omni-channel world

Customers interact with brands through a variety of devices and locations. These interactions depend on convenience and on each customer's individual schedule. An interaction that starts on a smartphone during a commute may continue on a desktop computer during the day, be expanded with a telephone call, and finished with a physical visit after work. Customers appreciate it when a conversation started in one location or channel continues seamlessly in the next channel, without the customer having to explain herself again in each new channel.

From the customer's viewpoint, a visit online on a smartphone is equal to a conversation with the clerk in a brick-and-mortar store. For the retailer, this seamlessness is difficult to achieve. It will require several opt-in confirmations by the customer, indicating that she really is OK with being tracked, as well as robust privacy guarantees by the retailer – but it can be done. It all depends on whether the information given by the customer is used only to improve the customer experience, or to spam the customer with irrelevant offers.

Again, the different channels and methods of interaction must be detailed on the customer journey map. Which devices do customers use? Which sources of information are likely to reach them? Where they come from, and where do they go after they leave your business? Using personas, you can get a good approximation of the truth. If you have data-mining capabilities, you can complement the customer journey with statistical information.

How do customers feel?

In addition to the interactions between the customer and the brand, an on-going emotional journey takes place within the customer. A map of this journey shows how customers feel at different stages and in different channels. At each point of interaction, we can map how personas feel: good, sad, frustrated, angry, happy, elated. Again, with data-mining and online services, you can easily see where people become unhappy and consider walking away from your business. Using personas and careful mapping, it is now possible to understand not only "how" characters feel, but also "why" they feel the way they do.

The goal of service design is to deliver a positive customer experience. On a basic level, that means removing sources of irritation from customer's path during all stages of his or

her journey.

Visualization and non-linear information

One of the most striking ways service design differs from typical business consultation is in the use of visualization. All information in a service-design analysis is presented as visually as possible because this makes information contextual and easy to understand in just a glance or two. It can be difficult to gain an overview of a book and see how everything fits together, but people can process images quickly and easily. A map containing significant amounts of information is immediately comprehensible and can present both general and specific data simultaneously. Furthermore, visual information in large formats can be viewed by groups of people together, thus leading to collaboration and sharing of information and experiences. Looking at a map, everyone is on the same page because there is only one page. Miscommunication is reduced.

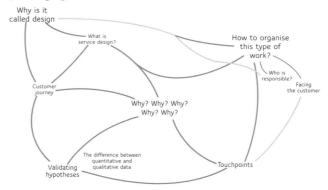

Complaints

The fact that no one is complaining does not mean that everyone is happy (and no, it doesn't mean that anyone is unhappy either). However, most consumers — over 90% of them — don't complain, often because they think venting their frustrations is a waste of time and will cost more than the complaint is worth. These customers show their unhappiness by not returning.

This is true for private companies but even more so for public services, where the public often feels powerless to change anything. Complaining to the tax department official, for example, may just cause more problems rather than a change of behavior on the part of the official.

Therefore, if one customer complains about a specific issue, you can bet that nine more customers have the same problem but haven't spoken up. So how do your customers feel? It isn't a trivial question. It is vital knowledge.

Validating hypotheses

Talking to people

You know a lot about your business that your customers don't care to know. Basing improvements in your service on what you know can create more problems than it solves. The biggest assumption is made in the beginning: we always presume that the customer is interested in our service or product. In fact, the opposite is often true. The customer's interest is often limited to wishing that the company would deliver a relevant service or product. Service delivered does not automatically equal value received.

> Service delivered ≠ value received

It is tempting to presume that a small sampling is indicative of all customers. Business owners often think that once things are explained in writing, changes won't have to be made because people can read the instructions and learn. The exercise in mapping customer journeys for many different personas utilizing many different channels should serve to illustrate how potentially complex situations can be.

Furthermore, this exercise should caution everyone to not make the mistake of presuming that a sample of one or two is indicative of the whole group. Jumping to conclusions like these is perhaps the most universal practice there is. To dispel the notion of "I saw it, therefore it must be true," read Daniel Kahneman's Thinking, Fast and Slow and The Black Swan by Nassim Nicholas Taleb.

Armed with the journey maps of various personas, we are well equipped to hypothesize what the most valuable aspects of the service or product are for the customers. We should also be able to predict which aspects are not important to them. We can now ask very intelligent questions. Therefore, the time is right to talk to customers.

It is imperative to have conversations with real people: frequent customers, former customers, fans, fans of other brands, and occasional customers. This is qualitative research, where time is taken to have conversations. This is not a multiple choice, fill-in-the-blank question-and-answer session but a conversation based on situations described in the hypothetical customer journey that, with the aid of the real customer, can be validated or amended or rejected.

How many conversations should you have? As many as necessary until the answers start repeating themselves. That's when you know that you've discovered a truth. However, there is a law of diminishing returns to take into account, which states that most issues are uncovered with few people. Beyond this point, having more conversations will only add to the quantity of answers but do nothing to change the quality.

For website-usability testing, Tom Landauer and Jakob Nielsen proved that it takes only 5 tests to reveal most of the issues around a website.

Nielsen Norman Group.
Why you need to test with 5 users.
http://tinyurl.com/a9ldz7d

how to have your cake and eat it too

The supermarket

Competition among supermarkets is largely price-based. The goods on sale are usually identical or very similar. The stores themselves vary only in interior ambience, layout, and location. All of them have a customer loyalty scheme, which rewards customers with reduced prices. The supermarket companies are large, and the central principles of each supermarket "concept" are fairly well defined. The logistics and marketing needs of these corporations are already well taken care of. However, innovation for improving the customer experience hasn't really happened. The whole customer journey, from empty refrigerator all the way back home with groceries in hand, has rarely been considered. The number of goods on sale has increased manifold over the last 20 years. The time constraints on our lives have also increased, and pressure on the household budget since the great recession has been startling. It is in this environment that home delivery of groceries, with pre-determined menus, is starting to disrupt the traditional model of driving to the supermarket and driving home. Many people – especially families with children – dread these twice-weekly trips to the supermarket and are in search of alternatives.

Self-scanning has reduced the time spent in the store. It finally enables customers to go through the store in the right order, immediately scanning and packing each item, so as to have the lettuce on top and the beer on the bottom. Also, it avoids the time-consuming routine of putting items in the trolley, removing them at the checkstand, and putting them back in the trolley for the walk to the car.

The food industry will never be completely automated. We want and need to see what we are buying before we buy it.

Home delivery is one alternative, but it can be hard for customers to coordinate their own needs and desires with the company's delivery schedule.

Each supermarket is organized somewhat differently, and customers become irritated when they have to navigate an unfamiliar store. The stores have solved this problem with signs, which they expect you will read before you enter each aisle. People, however, usually read instructions only if things don't work, which by definition means that they already have a problem making their customer journey unpleasant. Many supermarkets are also afflicted with staff shortages, so customers can't always find someone to help them and may go home without an item they needed or wanted.

The difference between quantitative and qualitative data

There is a presumption that only research encompassing a representative number of customers is valid – preferably dozens of questions asked of thousands of customers. However, if business owners are surprised by the answers from quantitative research, they should consider the possibility that they don't know their customers very well and should seek to understand these unexpected answers and the people who provided them. The fact remains, that by asking thousands of people questions you probably won't gain any insight whatsoever, whereas talking to just a few people in depth will give you dozens of new thoughts.

Businesses love quantitative data. Companies can hire researchers to collect and organize the data. When it is presented in colorful charts and graphs, it is often viewed as truth. Best of all, it often proves the obvious, which therefore ticks all the boxes of being reliable, timely and massive – therefore true.

Unfortunately, quantitative customer research describes the past and reports only what customers remember doing and thinking. In developing services and products that people value, we must focus on the underlying need that the product or service satisfies – the "why." This is rarely, if ever, uncovered in quantitative research involving thousands of disinterested parties.

Big data provides reams of quantitative information about past actions. Banks have tons of information on what customers paid for and when. However, they don't know why these items were paid for, what they were used for, and why these expenses were important to the customer in that moment. Often they see only whether or not a purchase was a propor-

Weak signals / fringes

Most people are not very concerned with individual brands; they look for convenience and usually choose the quickest and easiest route to what they want. They are not particularly interested nor particularly loyal. A customer who goes to the same store every week usually does so because of the store's location, not because of the products the store offers.

To understand what is really good (and really bad) about your business, you need to talk to your fans – and to those who have actively chosen not to patronize your business. Talking to these two customer groups is helpful because they KNOW why they love you or hate you. Strong feelings like these are signs of commitment and investment. These individuals probably even have ideas about how to improve your business.

Weak signals are another interesting place to look for insight. Customers who pick an item up in the early stages of its existence and can already see where it will go can offer incredible opportunity for insight into what will happen and why – they can almost predict the future. There is an adoption curve for everything. Seek advice from your product's earliest users; these individuals tend to be five steps ahead of other consumers and can see beyond the technology to the human needs your product will fulfill. Weak signals research can uncover trends before they go mainstream and help to position you to take maximum advantage of a paradigm shift.

tional expense considering the customer's income, and they may use the information to flag customers for economically inappropriate behavior.

Quantitative research is useful to confirm purchasing trends, but qualitative research is essential for companies that seek insights into the thoughts and feelings of their customers.

Conversations

Talking with people can be:

- time consuming
- unstructured
- inspiring
- honest

The basis of the conversation is the concerns that have arisen during the mapping of the hypothetical customer journey. The goal is not only to validate or reject the hypotheses, but also to gain insight and understand why problems have occurred. The prerequisite for having these conversations is a broad and deep understanding of the topic, both to be able to lead the conversation as well as to be able to recognize key insights. Driving these conversations has to be someone who is versed in all aspects of the service design project.

Important note: Empathy.
People tend to defend their positions. In organizing conversations, it is crucial that the mediator not defend the company's activities and position. The customer has the right to his or her opinion, and these opinions have nothing to do with how the business sees itself. There is NO right and wrong. To have successful conversations with customers,

One-to-one interviews

The advantage of one-on-one conversations is that they are intimate and relatively quick. It doesn't take much more than 1–2 hours to work through a complete customer journey with a customer, to understand whether the key hypothesis that you formulated applies to this person or not.

The best conversation partner is the one that listens. Your role in the conversation is to keep the dialogue flowing; the customer's role is to provide information to you. People are

experts in their own experience. When they have a chance to talk, they will do so, often going into great detail. However, when you ask direct questions, people tend to rationalize. As a result, you will get only an interpretation of past events, not a description.

Group discussions

Having a larger group of similar people in a group conversation has the benefit of bringing lots of opinions to the table. Conversations and ideas bounce off one another, and this process can be inspiring. The danger is of course that if someone dominates the conversation, everyone else will amplify this one person's opinion. The whole exercise can end up as completely irrelevant, if it isn't managed carefully.

Depending on the size of the group, you may have to divide it into smaller clusters of people. The best group size is three people, because no one can hide in such a small unit. In large groups, 1–2 people often end up dominating the conversation while the rest follow.

Allow for 3–4 hours for a group discussion. Ensure that everyone has an opportunity to contribute and feel valuable. It is important to realize that this kind of meeting is also a brand-building exercise where the brand directly interacts with customers and asks for advice. Make sure the tone of the meeting is serious.

Workshops

Knowing where problems lie is only half the battle. Knowing what to do about them is the other half. Working with a larger group of customer representatives to understand and validate or reject a customer journey hypothesis can also be part of the process of solving problems. People naturally have opinions not only of what is wrong but also of how the problem could be solved, for them. Therefore, with good crowd management it is possible to do two things at once: validate or reject a hypothesis and gain ideas on how to improve and fix problems.

Note that to have an effective co-creation workshop with customers, you have to understand clearly what you can gain from this kind of collaboration. Ideas are worth nothing without execution, and the group in the workshop is neither responsible for nor in a position to understand the details of execution. Their role is to suggest what ought to be done, not to decide how it should be done. The whole exercise loses meaning if the latter burden is also placed on participants. At this stage, the goal is still simply to gather high-quality information.

Data mining based on insight

When the conversations are over, it is valuable to focus data mining on key issues brought up in each conversation. Armed with the reason why, the "what" can be explored in detail, helping to define nuances and provide quantitative evidence to the qualitative insight. This use of data can also help to convince naysayers inside the organization that the issues need to be tackled.

Workshop 101

Depending on the size of the group, you may have to divide it into smaller clusters of people. The best group size is three people, because no one can hide in such a small unit. In large groups, 1-2 people often end up dominating the conversation while the rest follow.

Allow for plenty of time to explore the issues. While the goal of the exercise should always be clear, don't exert too much control if the crowd veers off course. If the discussion isn't fun, then people will not be willing to help.

Co-creation places some of the responsibility of a brand's development in the customers' hands. It also gives them the right to know what happens next. Follow up with your workshop participants periodically. Thanks to your hard work, you now have brand evangelists, who actually do care about the future of the company.

Each format for validating information is valuable and works well. Which one to use depends on the situation at hand.

Observation

People buy what is for sale. This means that people can't buy what is not on the shelf. So when asking people what they want, the most common answer is a request for something that is already out there. Therefore, one of the best ways of finding out what people actually have trouble with, and what is no trouble at all, is observation. Spend some time looking at what customers do and when they do it. Take notes. It is important though, that the observer doesn't influence the choice of the observed. Otherwise the whole exercise is moot.

People have a habit of taking short-cuts

Landscaping around new buildings often means that the walkways and sidewalks are predetermined and follow a route that looked good on a map when the building was being planned. However, if there is a shorter route between two points, a new path often appears in the place where people actually walked. Eventually, architects learned that landscaping before these natural walkways had been determined was a gigantic waste of money. Therefore, when larger buildings with large landscaping areas are finished, instead of proceeding according to the map, the area is simply cleared and left as it is for a few weeks. After this period, it is easy to determine where the natural paths are and how the walkways should be placed.

Families like it simple and quick

The McDonald brothers opened their first restaurant in 1940. It attracted throngs of customers, with harried carhops serving up to 125 carloads at a time. Within the decade, though, Mac and Dick realized they had to revamp their restaurant or find a new line of work. Some of their best customers were families giving Mom a night off from the kitchen. But now these families were driving right past the restaurant, turned off by the loitering toughs that drive-ins attracted. Many of the remaining customers complained that the food got cold on the journey from kitchen to car.

So they cut the menu to only 25 items and standardized the burgers. They replaced carhops with service windows. Productivity enhancers like five-at-a-time milk shake mixers enabled them to turn around food orders quickly.

Source: Roger Martin, the design of business

Touchpoints

Where business meets customer

Brands interact with consumers at many points throughout the customer journey. A touchpoint is where one of these interactions happens. Many of these touchpoints are passive. Some are interactive, and some are active only in one direction or the other. Mapping all these interaction points is vital to understanding the complete picture of what customers actually see and experience.

Based on conversations with customers, business owners often quickly learn that little details, which may seem like a waste to companies, are actually the most important parts of the brand experience from the customer's point of view. For example, fashion companies neglect stylish labels at their peril. No matter how good a garment is, it is the label that conveys the image and importance of the brand. From a production viewpoint, labels are at best an afterthought.

In the 1980s, North American cars were lambasted for their lack of attention to detail. American engineers often  neglected such details as the way it felt to operate the car's switches, whereas Japanese manufacturers spent inordinate amounts of time to ensure that the feel of everything was right. The complaints about American cars had nothing to do a car's primary purpose of getting from point A to B – both Fords and Hondas ran well. Drivers wanted the feeling of a thought-through driving experience and disliked cars in which they sensed that the manufacturer didn't really care about the driver. Eventually, this attention to detail in the Japanese auto industry led to the Honda Accord becoming North America's best-selling car, displacing the Ford Escort. Subsequently, Ford cooperated with Mazda just to get the Escort to feel right.

The fact that the car worked reliably was the biggest part of the cost on the manufacturers' side.

From a customer perspective, the fact that the car worked was a hygiene factor.

This misunderstanding between customers and brands about what actually matters can be attributed to the relative cost and value of the function at hand – the difference between value delivered and value received. In the case of the Honda Accord above, from an engineering and investment point of view, the fact that the car worked reliably was the biggest part of the cost (and effort) on the manufacturers' side. From a customer perspective, the fact that the car worked was a hygiene factor. If it didn't work, it wouldn't even be considered. However, that which makes the difference between a good driving experience and a not-so-good-one are all the things that the customer interacts with directly in the cabin of the car. Touch and feel. Smells and sounds.

In order to deliver a good customer experience, the goal must be to transcend how the service or product works and consider what it means to its users.

how to have your cake and eat it too

Meanings

An excellent presentation by the famed Harvard professor Clayton Christensen explains how the purchase of a milkshake is completely unrelated to the what the fast food restaurant values in its milkshakes.

Innovation Summit '09, Clayton Christensen.
http://tinyurl.com/nmksocp

The meaning, the "why" that explains why people prefer one product over another, is also a source of loyalty for brands. Being able to meet the need of customers is invaluable in building a sustainable business. In many ways this is the difference in success between iPod and Zune. Both did the same "what," but only iPod met the "why" of simplicity. "Easy" and "fun" is what it means to customers.

Case study:
The meaning of the customer relationship

What or with whom exactly does the customer have a relationship? A bank considers itself to have a relationship with a customer if he or she has at least two bank products. Today, that would constitute a bank card and access to internet banking. In other words, almost all bank customers meet the criterion for a relationship with the company, and the bank has a relationship with nearly all of its customers.

Conversations with young bank customers (defined as those without familial obligations, under the age of 28) showed conclusively that these customers didn't see themselves as having a relationship with the bank. Their selection of bank was largely pre-determined by their parents, and they had made no conscious decision about using this or that service provider. All they did was keep THEIR money in that bank. The relationship was not with the bank, but with their own money.

Because they now handled all their transactions themselves via the internet bank, the young bank customers had a very hard time explaining to themselves the value of the various bank charges. "It's my money and I do everything" was a common response. These young customers did not see the bank employees as financial advisors who offered a valuable service. The bank was synonymous in their minds with their money. This is an example of a difference in value delivered vs. value received.

Touchpoints and activities

What happens at each touchpoint? What are the internal processes at each touchpoint? What precedes and follows each touchpoint, and how are the touchpoints interdependent? What department is responsible for the touchpoint? What happens when the customer has problems at this point? What is the process for handling problems?

For each and every touchpoint we must define what the company does to make this touchpoint exist. What are the processes that are followed to make it real? This definition should not be abstract (i.e., marketing) but very specific (Julie in marketing, John in production) and should indicate who has to sign off on decisions related to this touchpoint.

Furthermore, we must define a time frame for the touchpoint. We need to keep track not only of the time on the customer journey, but also of the time at which the touchpoint was actually created. In some cases years can pass before the customer encounters the touchpoint. For example, until recently the GPS systems in cars were based on maps made 3-5 years beforehand. Therefore the GPS screens in brand new cars were already out of date when the cars rolled off the production line. Drivers suddenly found themselves frustrated with a built-in piece of technology that could not be updated, as it should be. Manufacturers could, of course, provide several good reasons that the GPS systems were based on old maps, but for customers none are convincing.

From the Brand Channel:
Ford ran into problems with consumers over the last couple of years as subsequent generations of Sync In-Car Infotainment System became more complicated to operate and owners pushed back via third-party rating venues such as Consumer Reports. But Ford has worked hard to overcome those difficulties, and its latest moves with Sync represent an attempt to

re-assert itself in the pole position of a telematics revolution that is vastly reconfiguring the very notion of a car and which is drawing in not only automakers but also a wide range of tech companies in what Ford futurist Sheryl Connelly has called a 'quiet riot of innovation.'"

Note that the feedback loop from customers to Ford is outside the control of the company. There is no way to control negative feedback, nor are there ways to amplify positive comments without seeming either aloof or vain. The most important communication channel for promoting a product or service is now between customers themselves, with no more input sought or required from the brand.

> The most important communication channel for promoting a product or service is now between customers themselves

In mapping and defining each touchpoint it is important to consider what each point can be when analyzed individually. Customers have the luxury of comparing apples with oranges and are often correct, presuming another service provider, in a different field, has already resolved a problem more intuitively. As people's experience broadens with more and more services available to them, it is easy to see that some companies are genuinely customer oriented while others still adhere to rigid bureaucracy that hampers delivering good results.

how to have your cake and eat it too

Two perfect storms

Customers are getting smarter. They have more options than ever before. They are able to complain and make their complaints known like never before. When companies make mistakes along the customer journey, they can find out in very unpleasant ways. The FedEx delivery man who threw a TV monitor over a fence while delivering it was captured on a security camera and the film was placed on YouTube. United Airlines experienced customer ire when a band wrote a song about the fact that their guitar had been broken by UA and they weren't compensated for it. This video also went viral on YouTube.

FedEx Guy Throwing Computer Monitor.
http://tinyurl.com/cfm6o4l

This focus on the customer experience – the need to deliver a positive experience – is intensifying due to two perfect storms happening at the same time. The first storm is technology-driven: the mobile internet, the internet of things, big data, analytics, social media, collaborative innovation and cloud computing. The second storm is made up of real-world

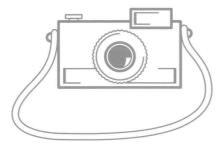

factors like global warming, biodiversity, globalization, urbanization, inequality and aging demographics, which are driving innovation.

These storms are empowering customers like never before. Industries are being disrupted by innovation that was impossible before the advent of the smartphone less than 10 years ago. In Who owns the future? Jaron Lanier stated that "at the height of its power, the photography company Kodak employed more than 140 thousand people and was worth $28 billion. Kodak even invented the first digital camera. Today Kodak is bankrupt and the face of digital photography has become Instagram. When Instagram was sold to Facebook for a billion dollars in 2012, it employed only 13 people." Instagram delivers a better, more immediate customer experience than Kodak could.

> The question is not in value delivered but value received.

The smartphone itself has become the most common camera, web browser, calendar, map, video camera, voice recorder, portable music player, calculator, photo album, emailing device, address book and clock. It simply provides a better customer experience than any of the above devices on their own – to a certain limit. It cannot replace a professional camera in the hands of a trained photographer. Nor can it match the simple versatility of pen and paper. But in 99 cases out of 100, it is good enough. The "killer app" of the smartphone is not that it does any of the above things better than dedicated mono-functional tools, but the fact that it is always with us. It allows for spontaneity, whereas carrying a photo album and voice recorder along requires planning.

Good enough is important to keep in mind, when reviewing the touch-points and how they fit in the customer journey. Again, we should focus not on value delivered but on value received. We should focus on questions like where the value received is highest – and where, consequently, scrutiny is

how to have your cake and eat it too

highest as well. This is where the customer experience has to be perfect. Elsewhere, "good enough" may in fact be enough.

Case study: McDonald's fame comes from having a standardized menu, consistent quality, good marketing, and a myriad of other factors. But the reason many people preferred McDonald's to other competition (both local and global brands), was McDonald's focus on cleanliness. In particular, the toilets were always clean. This fact, seemingly unrelated to the food served, makes a big difference when parents decide where to go to feed their kids fries. Psychologically, a clean toilet suggests that the kitchen is clean and the food is safe. Clean bathrooms make the whole customer journey through the restaurant pleasant.

Drawing the touchpoint matrix

There is no single best way to illustrate the customer journey with the touchpoints laid out at each stage. The level of detail depends on the product and service at hand. The following method has the benefit of being infinitely scalable and collaborative. As service design is a collaborative process, it is important that everything not rest on the shoulders of one person. Instead, cooperation between all the stakeholders is essential.

The simplest method is to draw out the detailed and proven customer journey on a very large piece of paper and paste it on a wall. With sticky notes each touchpoint is marked, defined and expanded.

Alternatively, it is possible to use a computer-based method – just make sure to use a collaborative platform. Proprietary software that is handled by one person will end up reflecting only that person's opinion.

Touchpoint Matrix

	Attract What is getting the customer's / user's attention	Choose What are we doing to make choosing the product / service eas
Stage / Place Where is it happening? Online or real life?		
Audience / Customer What is the customer doing?		
Actors / Staff What are staff doing?		
Script / Protocol What processes or procedures are being followed		
Backstage / Support functions What tools do staff have to work with		

e

t's going on when they
the product / service

Support

What makes using the
service / product better

Retain

What are we doing to make
sure the customer comes back

Differentiate between external and internal processes

The matrix is best considered like a play: the consumers are the audience. The actors are people or devices directly interacting with the customer. The script is the procedure being followed. The stage is the setting where things happen. Backstage are the processes that are invisible to the customer. The plot of the play reflects the customer journey. The reasons behind these actions have to do with what is happening backstage and are usually invisible to the customer. The purpose of this work is to describe, define and explain why things are done the way they are, how these processes affect the customer journey and what can and should be done to improve the customer experience by changing, removing, or improving backstage activities.

Iterations

Although the process herein is described as linear, it may not be. Each step can require new validation with customers or a review of what happens inside the company at each touchpoint. Design as a methodology requires continuous scrutiny of principles. When the answers seem to be perfect, it is possible that we are asking the wrong questions. The determination to seek and consider the customer's viewpoint at every step will keep the process from going off track.

How to organise this type of work?

Who is responsible?

Providing a better experience at all touchpoints along the customer journey requires the organization to take a look at the whole picture. It is not the responsibility of the marketing department or UX design in the web department or of visual merchandising in-store. Instead, it is the responsibility of the CEO, because changes in departmental and inter-departmental work will most likely be needed. Conventionally, it is only the boss who can ensure that politics and departmental self-interest don't overrule common-sense solutions.

Maybe the business is too big for the CEO to do this personally. Nevertheless, this process will require someone (or many people) to work broadly across departments in order to reap the benefits of service design methods. Eventually, budgets will need to be re-allocated and priorities in product and service development reviewed and maybe revised.

Service design organizes business from the customer's perspective.

To organize business is the responsibility of the board.

"The purpose of business is to create and keep a customer."

Peter F. Drucker

Who is involved? All stakeholders.

This key principle cannot be over-emphasized or said too much. All stakeholders are involved in the service design process, and the customer must be in the center. At the end of the day, the customer is the one who is paying for the product or service; therefore, anything that is done which increases customer satisfaction in the long term is worth doing.

Complexity

Delivering a product or service often requires management of complexity. Businesses, especially larger ones, have turned to bureaucracy to manage complexity. Bureaucracy forces everyone to tick boxes and follow rigid processes in order to deliver a consistent product or service.

As new services or products are developed, they are layered on top of old ones, which creates even more complexity. One way or the other, customers are forced to deal with this complexity and may become frustrated. The only reason that it has been tenable for so long to force customers to deal with complexity, is that your competitors have been doing largely the same thing. No one has stopped to ask "why" things are the way they are.

Today, as people have more and more interaction with various services and products (which may be for different uses but inherently work the same way) they also compare notes with one another on what it was like to deal with various companies. Companies deemed too complicated will likely lose business, and companies that receive more positive reviews will gain customers rapidly.

Compare the relative unease of government services to the quickness and simplicity of Google, for example. As customers become more aware of their choices, they legitimately ask "why" some service experiences are as bad as they are, if they aren't so bad elsewhere.

Turning this problem around means charting the customer journey and understanding where value (for the cus-

SCALING

REQUIRES

FOR MANAGING
RISK — PROCEDURES — FOR CREATING
PROFIT

WHICH
CREATE

COMPLEXITY

WHICH IS
MANAGED
BY CREATING

PRODUCTS
BASED ON

AGE   LOCATION   INCOME   PROFESSION

THAT HAVE TO BE
COMMUNICATED

LANGUAGE
LIKE

CONCEPTS   SYMBOLS   JARGON

THAT HAVE TO BE
EXPLAINED

TO ALL GROUPS DIFFERENTLY

WHICH
CREATES

tomer) is actually created. And then simplifying everything so that the value is delivered as quickly and easily as possible.

Simplicity means making decisions

Mono-functional tools are the best. A carving knife is better for carving than a pocket knife. A real camera is better than a smartphone. A flight ticket booking site where it is possible to just book the tickets and understand exactly what you're paying for is better than a site that also offers you hotels, taxis, buses, insurance, and coffee on board.

Over time, simple tools get complicated if one forgets where the value lies for the customer. At one time, Nokia was the best mobile phone maker, providing simple, intuitive menus that everyone could learn to use in minutes. However, with each new phone, new layers of possibilities were added to the menu, without considering if it were necessary to omit older functionalities.

> It easier not to choose than to try to choose among a multitude of incomprehensible versions

Eventually, users were required to move their Nokia phones through five levels of completely unintuitive menus just to change the ring-tone. Shortly thereafter, along came the iPhone with a learning curve of 30 seconds.

Simplicity means reducing the number of options, not increasing them. Simplicity means making some decisions for the customer, not deferring everything so that she can choose. Having many options to choose from has been shown to cause stress and actually turns people away. Many users find it easier not to choose than to try to choose among a multitude of incomprehensible versions of the same basic product.

Does choice facilitate buying?

When researchers Mark Lepper and Sheena Iyengar set up a display in a gourmet food store featuring a line of exotic, high-quality jams, customers who came by could taste samples and were given a coupon for a dollar off if they bought a jar. In one condition of the study, six varieties of the jam were available for tasting. In another, 24 varieties were available. In either case, the entire set of 24 varieties was available for purchase. The large array of jams attracted more people to the table than the small array, though in both cases people tasted about the same number of jams on average. When it came to buying, however, a huge difference became evident. Thirty percent of the people exposed to the small array of jams actually bought a jar; only three percent of those exposed to the large array of jams did so.

Build up confidence

When the work has been done to map the whole customer journey and the touchpoint matrix, the results can seem a little daunting. A whole slew of issues will have likely cropped up that should be worked on, and coordinating all of this data can look like a nightmare.

Therefore, it is best to take small steps. It is important to build up the company's confidence in the belief that this approach is reasonable and worthwhile. Improve and change the easiest pieces first and measure the before and after effect. By demonstrating through small initiatives that improving the customer experience pays rapid dividends, the organization accepts the need for larger changes much more easily. Furthermore, large changes require inter-departmental cooperation, which may require a change in how the business is organized in the first place.

Facing the customer

Small businesses have the luxury of meeting their customers often. When employees interact with customers, they can empathise with them. Large organizations with hundreds of thousands or millions of customers have armies of employees engaged in work that has no direct connection to the customer. Eventually, organisations may re-orient themselves to face not the customer, but internal metrics which have nothing to do with value for the customer or their experiences with the service.

Knock, Knock, Nokia's Heavy Fall

Nokia has lost its way. What on earth happened to the mobile phone pathfinder?

This article is reprinted with the kind permission of Helsingin Sanomat and the author Mikko-Pekka Heikkinen. First published in the Kuukausiliite monthly supplement for October 2010

The woman who pours the coffee has asked that her name and location not be published in this article. The subject around the coffee table is the handset manufacturer Nokia, the woman's former employer. She worked for Nokia for more than 25 years, but is now retired.

Nokia is not doing too well. The company's stock has taken a huge hit, competitors are making finer phones that are finding their way into more pockets, and Nokia's Finnish CEO was given his marching orders last month. What on earth has happened to the company? It is a sensitive subject, and hence the plea for anonymity. During her working career she worked at a Nokia production plant where mobile phone handsets were assembled.

In a vast hall, processor, memory, microphone, battery, keyboard, and all the bits and pieces were packed by hand into mobile phones. Finally, the shell of the newly-minted phone was snapped shut, and the employee moved on to the next one. The woman reports that a change began to take place within Nokia five years ago, and it was visible all the way to the factory floor.

The change began when Olli-Pekka Kallasvuo became the Nokia President and CEO. He was appointed in 2005 and took up residence in his office from June 2006. During Kallasvuo's tenure, the Nokia plant became a colder, harder place. Employees were not trusted as much as they had been, but rather their work began to be strictly monitored. Line supervisors were controlling even the grip that was to be used when assemblers fitted the components into the handset shells.

how to have your cake and eat it too

In the view of the woman, a kind of "me-me-me spirit" had swept through Nokia. This paralysed creativity and displaced the strong sense of "us" solidarity that lifted the company in the 1990s onto the global mobile phone throne. The feeling of working together towards a common end has been eroded for instance by the fact that the senior management are no longer witnessed chatting with Nokia staff. This was by no means uncommon during the term of Jorma Ollila*. "Ollila came to the plant several times a year. He never announced when he would be dropping in. He didn't want any red carpet treatment or special preparations put in place for his visits," says the woman.

Ollila would stroll around on the factory floor, going from one assembly point to the next and stressing that he was "Just Jorma, please." "He might just stop at one employee's side and ask how he or she was getting on, what's the work like, and is there anything that is ticking you off," the woman goes on, and offers up another slice of pie. And if there were problems in the company or at the plant, Ollila knew how to gee people up. He spoke rousingly about "us" and delivered his message to the whole complement at the plant, not just to a small group as was Kallasvuo's way. Sometimes Ollila was accompanied by two of the most senior members of the Executive Board at that time – Pekka Ala-Pietilä and Matti Alahuhta. "They had a quite phenomenal ability to get people forged together behind the same cause. They created confidence and trust."

Since his departure, the management skills of the deposed Nokia CEO Olli-Pekka Kallasvuo have been the subject of direct, even blunt criticism. But can Nokia's recent decline be laid exclusively at Kallasvuo's door? No, it cannot. In years gone by a number of far-reaching decisions were made within Nokia. They had their own impact on the recent past, and on the fact that Nokia's achievements of late have remained so thin on the ground. The decisions were taken at the beginning of the century, in other words years before Kallasvuo got the keys to the CEO's office. The power in Nokia at that time rested with Chairman and CEO Jorma Ollila.

Nokia is still the world's largest manufacturer of mobile phone handsets, and by a country mile. One in every three mobile phones sold worldwide has the Nokia logo on it. Nokia sells more than a million handsets a day. From the 1990s to the early years of the new century,

*Nokia's President and CEO from 1992-1999, Chairman and CEO from 1999-2006)

Nokia grew to quite mind-boggling dimensions and numbers. In 2000, the company's market capitalization value was a dizzying €300 billion. In many markets, "Nokia" was at one time a direct synonym for the words "mobile phone" – it was the de facto term of choice, like "Hoover" for vacuum cleaner or "Xerox" for photocopies. The firm was the economic and technological miracle and stealth weapon with which Finland overcame the rest of the world, and above all the Swedes. Our beloved neighbor's own mobile phone giant Ericsson was steamrollered by the onrushing Nokia juggernaut. Finland rose phoenix-like from the ashes of the early 1990s recession with the help of Nokia's stunning growth figures.

In those days, Nokia was the pioneering name in mobile phones. As early as 1996, the company launched on the world a revolutionary device whose direct descendants are known today as smartphones. The Nokia 9000 Communicator became a watchword, with any number of affectionate nicknames. The clamshell device opened up to reveal an integrated QWERTY keyboard, and it came with a browser that even allowed rudimentary surfing of the internet. This was an earth-shaking new breakthrough at the time. The Communicator was among the first attempts at putting the Net into our pocket, albeit a bulging pocket.

In the first decade of the 21st century, the marrying of the mobile phone handset and the Net has become the decisive battle for hearts and minds in the mobile branch. It is no longer sufficient that a phone can be used to make calls or send SMS messages on the fly, but it must now enable the user to surf the Net, to Google all manner of human knowledge, and to regularly update his or her Facebook status. And in this battle, once-mighty Nokia has taken a pounding.

The mobile phone should not simply work, but it should also evoke warm feelings in the user. One executive who designed user interfaces for Nokia in the 1990s and into the new century stresses that a mobile is not a basic consumer durable like a washing machine or a fridge-freezer, but "a device towards which people have a very strong emotional attachment." "Devices like this should be made with the heart and in some fashion as hand-crafted items," he says. In the years of its pomp, Nokia and its engineer-powered machinery swelled to colossal proportions. According to the former manager, there was an adverse consequence to this unbridled expansion: "The hand-crafted sense of the products melted away."

A challenger to Nokia's hegemony in the mobile phone business came from the United States. In the summer of 2007, the California-based computer manufacturer Apple launched onto the U.S. market its multimedia smartphone, the iPhone, in the wake of the phenomenally successful iPod portable media player. It was a jaw-dropping device on its appearance. On the face of the futuristic, shiny black slab there was just one physical menu button. Pressing this brought up a large display screen featuring brightly-colored icons. By touching these with a finger, as if by magic the screen lit up with a touch-sensitive virtual keyboard, a web browser, SMS messages, email, maps, a calendar, a digital camera, and a built-in media player.

And for the first time in the short and hectic history of mobile devices, using all these properties was simplicity itself. In fact it was more than easy – it was fun. There was no need to pore over manuals to be able to change the ringtone or to find the URL address line in the browser. The graphics on the touch-screen responded to the movement of a finger sensitively and seductively, and text or picture scrolled back and forth as if adhering to the laws of gravity and friction. The user's first close encounter with the iPhone produced a spontaneous WOW effect.

One former Nokia employee says that within the company the initial reaction to Apple and its iPhone was dismissive: They don't know how to make phones, now do they? According to another, the iPhone was a serious wake-up call and lesson for the Nokia family.

The game got a whole lot tougher from the middle of the following year. In July 2008, Apple opened up its online App Store, which sold – and gave away – a range of software applications for the iPhone that could be downloaded directly to the user's individual device. Some were just silly toys, like the swishing sound-effects for a Star Wars lightsaber that responded to the hand movements of the phone's owner, or an image of a buzzing virtual electric shaver that filled the display screen. Daft perhaps, but they made people laugh. Since then, a vast array of mobile games, services, and utilities have been added to the App Store assortment – more than a quarter of a million third-party applications at the last count in September 2010.

Anyone and everyone can install them on the phone, and many of the add-on programs are quite mind-bogglingly ingenious. One augmented reality application, for instance, uses GPS and gyroscope technology to draw on the screen an accurate star-chart of the night sky when the device is directed towards the heavens. In essence, "you point at a corner of the sky and it shows you what's up there." With things like this offered either for free or for a few euros apiece, it is hardly any wonder that something like 6.5 billion downloads from the App Store have been recorded to date.

Nokia began selling applications for its own phones as early as in 2003. The current digital distribution platform for these things is the online Ovi service, which was announced at a gaming event in London in August 2007. Ovi has nevertheless not been anything like as successful as the App Store. The Ovi Store assortment of mobile games, maps, applications, audio and video media, and other widgets is a fraction of the size of that in App Store, and some customers have complained that the service is not overly user-friendly in practice. Ovi has been a disappointment to consumers, the developers of applications, and Nokia investors alike.

Apple usurped Nokia's former position as the mobile device pathfinder. The company dug up the entire playing field and reseeded it. Apple was the first to merge successfully mobile telephony, the Net, and a range of useful or entertaining applications into a single easy-to-use device that fits neatly into any hand or pocket. In the words of one former Nokia Vice-President: "Apple has only gone and done those things that were envisioned by Nokia, but which Nokia has itself been unable to bring into the real world."

Apple also resolved the thorny "naming of parts" problem that had pestered the marketing of the new generation of intelligent mobile devices, points out one manager who designed user interface software for Nokia. From the 1990s, Nokia had been trying to come up with a suitable catch-all term for these devices. There were clumsy names, as clunky as the first "shoebox" phones of the 1980s, like "mobile multimedia computer." Apple had no truck with this, but announced that its device was simply "a phone." "The iPhone is certainly no phone. It is a pocket computer, but one you can make calls with," says the ex-VP.

Now Apple Inc. has a market value many times that of Nokia. Apple's market capitalization is currently of the order of €190 billion, while Nokia's has shrunk to approximately €30 billion, a far cry from the

how to have your cake and eat it too

heyday of 2000. According to the Nordea Bank, Apple today accounts for as much as 60% of the annual profit made by the entire mobile device branch. In the space of three years it has snatched up 14% of the global smartphone market. In the same period, Nokia's market share in this sector has declined from 50% to 41%.

Why is it that Nokia, once the undisputed king of the hill, has not come up with a device that matches the allure of the iPhone? One answer to this conundrum is provided by a man who worked for more than ten years at the top end of Nokia's product development arm.

A waiter brings over a latte and a crème brûlée. Across the table in the cafeteria at Helsinki's high-end Hotel Kämp sits a man who looks like he must be an engineer. He, too, prefers not to have his name in print. The former product development executive spoons up a piece of the dessert and begins: "In the 1990s Nokia's product development was still very much concentrated on one product – or at the most two products – at any given time. Every product had a clearly-defined team working on it, where the people focused on that one item and no others." Hit mobile phones emerged and went into production. Devices that many people remember even today, such as the 2110 or the 6110, with its infrared port and menu icons. Then along came 2000, and thereafter a decision was taken to increase the number of available Nokia handsets. "Two new models a year was no longer enough, but there was a perceived need to bring out as many as 40 or 50 models a year. An utterly terrifying number."

The old teamwork way of doing things no longer worked in this climate, because it would not have been effective. A decision was made to establish so-called component workshops that would build functions for phones across the old-model demarcation lines. Phones began to be constructed by ordering up selected functions – for example an onboard camera application – from the component workshops. "This really was an effective way of working. But at the same time it meant the loss of a product-centered approach, and we forgot what the firm was actually selling – mobile phones for people," says the former manager. "The products became characterless, standard fare devices; phones cobbled together out of basic components and not really differing one from another in any meaningful way. And the wild ideas and visions were killed off effectively by the choking grip of factory thinking."

Apple's iPhone is an ingenious package of properties and technologies that Nokia had at its fingertips, or that it could have acquired just like Apple managed to do. But this did not happen. There has not even been a decent copy of the iPhone from Nokia, in spite of the fact that people have been expecting the Finns to serve one up for more than three years. What's been keeping them?

The former manager offers a graphic example of Nokia's product development "scrum" process from the early years of the decade. A designer responsible for the mobile phone's integrated digital camera works out how the picture quality could be improved by a change in algorithm that would demand a couple of weeks' work to sort out. He reports on this to his immediate superior, who then feeds the matter into the requirements analysis matrix. A week later the matter is noticed at an RA follow-up session and further information is sought: if this were to be done, what other things would be omitted or would come in behind schedule as a result? The team replies that their error-fixing capacity would temporarily be reduced. Another week goes by. The next RA follow-up session looks at the answer and decides to send the request on for prioritization.

After a week, the requirements are examined in a prioritization meeting, and a decision is made to go back to the team to check out the errors status, in order to be able to understand what the scale of risk involved in reducing error-fixing might be. The team comes up with a risk analysis in a day or two. Another week goes by. A prioritization meeting resolves to approve the initial request, if a suitable "lead product" can be found for it – in other words, a phone model into which the improved algorithm can be installed.

A month later, one product reports back that, yes, we could take the improvement on, if it does not add to the risk of a timebox overrun. Back to the team. Is there an increased risk of the timebox not being met? The team replies that no such risk exists if work is started straightaway. Another week goes by, and the prioritization meeting gives the second-highest priority to the camera request. It determines that the algorithm change can be embarked on, just as soon as any more important work has been completed.

The more important matters take two months. By the point when the algorithm team should then be getting down to work, it turns out that the scheduling of the lead product has progressed too far and

86

the timebox window has closed. Another lead product must be found instead. And so it goes on, until a competitor gets rave press reviews for the improved image quality of its integrated camera. And someone expresses shock, and wonders why it is that Nokia has not come up with a similar improvement.

The former product development manager sips his coffee and recalls his feelings: "It made you feel like shouting out: 'For Christ's sake, can't you just bloody DO it and stop all this passing the buck!'. And there were many chains of events just like this one, and worse besides." In other words, Nokia's product development process was bureaucratic, stiff, and painfully slow.

Another ex-Nokia executive confirms the thrust of the earlier remarks. He charges that there was all too much office politics in play in the company: "Individual profit centers have so much clout that they can change the direction of development. They have their own games to play out. They don't think of the best interests of the consumer, but of their own unit. Its role, its resources, and what products it gets to make."

In the Kämp Hotel café, the ex-R&D man talks about the battles that went on between the many and varied operating systems in Nokia phones. The operating system is the software that determines what is seen on the display screen and how the phone is used. "Sometimes one got the sensation that people were more concerned about how what we were doing and the product we were working on related to rival groups within the company than about the relationship to our real competitors. The products using a certain software platform were not permitted to implement the newest or the cleverest things, because this might make the device in question a competitor to some other Nokia phone using a different platform."

And now Nokia's Symbian platform is being seriously threatened by the proprietary iOS developed by Apple, and most recently by the open source, Linux-derived Android platform backed by Google. Google's multi-carrier Android OS has made a big splash and is gaining ground in particular in the mid-range smartphone market, for instance inside the mobiles produced by the South Korean manufacturer Samsung. At the very top end, Apple's iPhone continues to rule the roost.

The next person to be interviewed for this article is a man who has a lot to say. He worked in the past decade in middle management positions within Nokia, for example in user interface design, conceptualizing, and brand management tasks. He does not mince his words, and in his view the ranks of Nokia's middle and senior management are altogether too crowded. The foggy grey mass of the organization critical hinders the progress of the engineers' clever inventions towards their intended destination in mobile phone handsets.

The man recounts a "thoroughly typical" example: A novel application or feature has been dreamed up that should end up installed in a phone a year from now. This is the beginning of a long day's journey to nowhere. The first thing that is missing is the conceptualization of the feature in question, and then comes the design phase, and after that the bedding of the feature into the phone. People have to sign off on actions at every stage in the process for it to go forward. According to the ex-manager, everybody who knows anything about this particular feature approves of the idea, albeit with one or two modifications.

"But then you run up against some Vice-President who gets cold feet, because he doesn't know the subject-matter. The innovation is going to tie up money and resources if it gets the go-ahead. He is very aware of this, and he sits on it. He might for our purposes be an engineer with a background in HVAC or systems engineering. He doesn't know squat about user interface software design.

What he does know, mind you, is that developing this particular feature is going to require the input of fifty people for the next year ahead. He does not dare to commit people to the project, because they might be required elsewhere. For him, it is safer to freeze the innovation process or at least keep the handbrake on. Then in time the innovation will no longer be so novel after all, and it will not make any sense to carry it forward."

According to the ex-manager's own calculations, there are around 300 vice-presidents and SVPs within the Nokia organization. A hundred would probably be quite enough. "If the company goes on with the current structure, one thing is certain, and that is that nothing will ever change." For example inside Google, widely regarded as one of the world's most inventive enterprises, there is none of the expanding waistline found in the Nokia organization. Furthermore, Google actually makes a point of pricking its employees into coming up with all kinds of new ideas. The Google staffers can use a fifth of their working time on developing their own projects. Small shoots like these have grown up into things like Gmail and Google News.

The strength of Nokia's American competitors comes from managers who know what sort of products should be being made. And these managers also push to see them getting into production. "There are not the sort of strong figures within Nokia who can come out and say 'Hell yeah, we're going to do this and see it through, even if it takes us two or three years.' This is because the people in those management positions aren't up to the task. And that's why they are lacking in the necessary courage and backbone.

The members of the Nokia Board and the Group Executive Board are untrained people insofar as Nokia's present business is concerned. Neither the Board nor the Executive Board has a single representative who could broadly be described as a visionary type. It would be something if there were even one, but by rights there ought to be eight of them."

By "Nokia's present business," the ex-manager means that mobile phone manufacturers are no longer companies that turn out merely devices and hardware, but that they must also provide online services such as Ovi or Apple's App Store, which are used by the owners of those devices. The genesis in a company of services that are attractive to the customer and "sticky," in the sense of pulling the users in and holding them – like Facebook, for instance – is something that requires creative leadership. According to the ex-manager, this is something that Nokia has never been able to boast. "Managing technology can be done successfully as teamwork, but creative management doesn't work that way."

The man is thus pointing the finger squarely at Nokia's uppermost management echelon. Clearly there have been problems there, or otherwise it is hard to see why President and CEO Olli-Pekka Kallasvuo would have been set aside recently in favor of Stephen Elop, headhunted to the post from Microsoft's Business Division. But if we are to believe the former Nokia staffers and executives interviewed for this piece, Nokia's woes began years before Olli-Pekka Kallasvuo's tenure at the helm, back at the beginning of this decade. During Chairman and CEO Jorma Ollila's time. And in 2003, Ollila did something that put the Finnish mobile phone giant onto the wrong tracks.

On the table in the meeting room in downtown Helsinki are a few sticky buns, coffee cups, and a data projector. Into the room steps a man wearing a tailored sports jacket. He made a point of not wanting to meet in a café, so that nobody would see him talking to a reporter. He pulls the door to behind him.

The man sits himself down at the table and gives a quick run-through of his background: a long career at Nokia, with many years in an executive role. He witnessed at first hand Nokia's rise to become the world's largest manufacturer of mobile handsets. This all happened with a very simple corporate structure. As recently as at the beginning of the century, Nokia had just two business units: Mobile Phones making handsets and Nokia Networks producing cellular network equipment and solutions.

The former Nokia executive pours coffee. At that time, he says, Mobile Phones were in full gallop and it was Nokia, for all practical purposes. The unit generated 80% of the company's annual net sales. From 1998 it was headed by Matti Alahuhta as President. Alahuhta was a well-liked figure, even down on the assembly hall floor. Then everything changed.

In September 2003, Nokia announced it was comprehensively rearranging the corporate furniture, and Mobile Phones was broken up into three business groups: Mobile Phones, Multimedia, and Enterprise Solutions. Mobile Phones was given responsibility for basic phones "for large consumer segments," Multimedia was charged with "bringing mobile multimedia to consumers in the form of images, games, music and a range of other attractive content," and Enterprise Solutions was to provide "seamless mobile connectivity solutions" for business. In the considered view of the ex-Nokia man, "the key reason" for Nokia's present problems is there: Jorma Ollila's matrix organization, which came into effect from January 1, 2004.

The man pauses and raises the coffee cup to his lips. "What emerged was a leadership vacuum. Right there and then the seed of gradual internal decay was planted. The various units began to compete tooth and nail with each other for the same resources and the same markets. And above them there were not the necessary strong decision-making mechanisms for control of the product assortment. I mean the sort of leadership that would have looked at the big picture and held up a hand and said: 'Hey, just a second now, it doesn't make any sort of sense to manufacture overlapping products like this,'" says the former Nokia manager.

He takes the view that the restructuring of 2004 led to a situation where the management of the product assortment fell apart and the development of technologies shifted to become very short-sighted – a sort of "instant gratification" model. "People tried simply to respond to the challenges and needs of all the different product lines. There was not enough time and money for work at the long-haul end. For example for things like updating and upgrading the operating system software," he goes on. This lack of far-sighted research proved to be a significant stumbling block a few years down the line, when a competitor unleashed on the market a real humdinger of a touch-screen mobile phone.

"Precisely. Nobody had had the responsibility for thinking about and putting hands to work on the next user interface. Nokia woke up with its pants around its ankles when the iPhone arrived. In practice, nothing had been done about it at that point. It really was not anyone's direct responsibility in the then organization. The responsibility was spread about all over the place, in the whole house. All the resources at that time went into producing the existing product assortment."

This is not to say Nokia had no touch-screen technology. It did have. For example the Nokia 7710 multimedia smartphone, released in 2004 and "ahead of its time," came with a wide, touch-screen color LCD. However, the model worked and sold poorly, and was discontinued not long afterwards.

The former Nokia manager reports that the development of the touch-screen technology that went into the prototype 7700 and the 7710 model had to be wound up some time in 2005, or two years before the advent of the iPhone. The sums of money that were going into the product development were being drained away from maintaining an assortment comprising dozens of handsets that were all much of a muchness one with another.

"The development of the touch-screen should have been continued," argues the man. "All the most catastrophic errors are associated with decision-making on the product management side. We produced a quite enormous number of rather average products. It would have been smarter to make fewer – and better."

The ex-manager charges that Nokia has the world's most ineffective product development regime. It is possible to examine this claim in the light of some recent numbers: between April and June of this year Nokia spent a heap of money – some €737 million – on product development. This was more than twice as much as was spent by Apple.

On the other hand, Nokia's Devices and Services unit generated just €647 million in operating profit for Q2/2010, or approximately €2.7 billion less than Apple for the same period. Nokia's top-floor management did not notice quite how frenzied the competition between the business units had become. "Jorma Ollila neither saw nor understood the enormous degree to which the organisation had become politicised from within."

Just as it had been at the turn of the century, Nokia Mobile Phones was also the most important of the company's business units at the time of the next re-organisation in 2004. The Chairman and CEO of Nokia Jorma Ollila had chosen the firm's then EVP and Chief Financial Officer Olli-Pekka Kallasvuo to head the division. This was a move into the elevator to the big office. Two years later, Kallasvuo was appointed as Ollila's successor at the helm of the company.

In the meeting room in downtown Helsinki, the former Nokia manager pours more coffee as if to steel himself. Olli-Pekka Kallasvuo is spared even fewer plaudits from his direction than were forthcoming for Ollila. Kallasvuo is a lawyer by training, and he joined the company in 1980 as Corporate Counsel. In the late 1980s he was made AVP in the Legal Department, and shortly afterwards took on similar tasks on the finance side of the business. One other former Nokia executive describes him as "an extremely good manager, but a poor leader," who has difficulty getting the staff to follow his flag.

The ex-manager notes over his coffee that Kallasvuo, coming from the CFO's position, was lacking in experience of the operative management of a large corporation. "Kallasvuo didn't understand the first thing about how the corporation should be organised or how it should work. A product-driven company, in which the product is no longer a piece of hand-held hardware but rather the experience of the user." In the years that followed, Kallasvuo made his own organizational reshuffles. They left the company even more hamstrung than the moves made by Ollila in late 2003.

"They took the organization in an ever more confused and confusing direction and created a kind of internal impotence. Ultimately nobody knew who was making the decisions and about what. This leads in practice to a situation where there are a great many heads that can shake and say 'No,' but not many who can say 'Yes, and this is how we are going to do it,'" says the former Nokia manager. "The real responsibility and the place where the buck stops is altogether too high up the chain. The individual who can say 'Yes' is no less than a personage than the CEO."

By contrast with the brickbats dealt out for the management structure, the former manager has nothing but praise for the people working at the coal-face, Nokia's engineers. "Nokia has a complement of totally outstanding engineers! It's not down to their skills. But it is the product management side of things that has been so weak and so diffused. And the CEO ought to have recognized this. There should have been a product director. And a strong one at that. But there was none." So neither Jorma Ollila nor Olli-Pekka Kallasvuo was the sort of corporate water-bringer for the 2010s that Apple enjoyed in its own CEO, Steve Jobs.

The ex-Nokia manager gets up from the table and straightens his jacket. The working day is getting under way, and the time set aside for this interview is up. The original causes of Nokia's recent fall from grace are beginning to become clear. But the information gained needs to be put to some kind of bench-test. We will have to drink some more coffee, but this time not in the company of former executives and managers.

The woman with whom we talked some weeks ago lifts her cup periodically and nibbles on a biscuit. She pores intensively over a text on sheets of A4. The woman, now retired after working for more than 25 years at a Nokia production facility, has been given this article to read through shortly before it goes to print. She reaches the last page and tidies the papers with a sigh. "Well, there you go."

"Yes, this is just the sort of picture that I had – what these product development people have been saying here. Totally. I mean, where things started to go wrong." The woman repeats the claims made in the article. She agrees on many points, even though she has not formed her opinions at a desk in the mobile phone giant's head office in Espoo, but on the assembly line.

Then the woman says something that is rather interesting. Even CEO Jorma Ollila was less than enthusiastic about the heavy organizational structure, and recognized perfectly well that it was making Nokia stiff and sluggish in its movements. In their time, Ollila's views made it all the way down to the factory floor.

But was it not Jorma Ollila himself who created the organization he led? "Yes," replies the woman. Ollila's unwavering line was to allow his subordinates freedom, to trust them without tight controls. In this way the then leaders of the business units like Mobile Phones and Multimedia could recruit whom they wanted. And in so doing the number of managers at all levels mushroomed to enormous proportions and the product development channels became clogged.

A total of fifteen former Nokia employees were interviewed for this article. Olli-Pekka Kallasvuo and Jorma Ollila did not wish to comment on the claims that were put forward.

Why is this article here?

Nokia's rise and fall should be a wake-up call to every company never to lose sight of the customer. This article reads like fiction, but is more likely the truth for many a conglomerate around the world. Bill Clinton is famous for saying "it's the economy, stupid." For businesses "it's the customer, stupid" should be the focus. Every time this principle is forgotten, for the sake of the Excel table, it has dire consequences.

It is about people

Service design improves the customer experience, and a company that seeks to improve the customer experience must first understand its customers. Before that, we must understand the people involved in delivering the product or service.

We must understand underlying motivations, which at the end of the day means that to do service design, we must be good at understanding people.

> Only compromises are based on rational decision criteria. Other decisions are emotional.

There is a fair amount of psychology involved, and we must begin by accepting from the outset that people aren't machines. People are emotional, though they sometimes make compromises based on rational criteria. Other decisions are emotional and based on feelings, or the weather, or if a certain football team won yesterday, and so on. This applies to customers as well as staff.

To motivate both staff and customers, it makes good sense to have a purpose that is above and beyond just making money. Earning profit for a company isn't motivating for customers. Earning money for the boss isn't a good reason to put in extra effort.

Roles in the process

It takes two to tango, but only one can lead. The design process starts with the fuzzy front end, where we are looking for information in general without knowing where it will lead us. There are people who are comfortable in leading this kind of research work, and those that are not. It is important to understand and assign roles in this process. Someone has to lead. Others provide information.

Service design follows a process. Those that understand the process must lead. Those that have information must be allowed to provide it without judgment. It is up to the process

Design Process & Roles

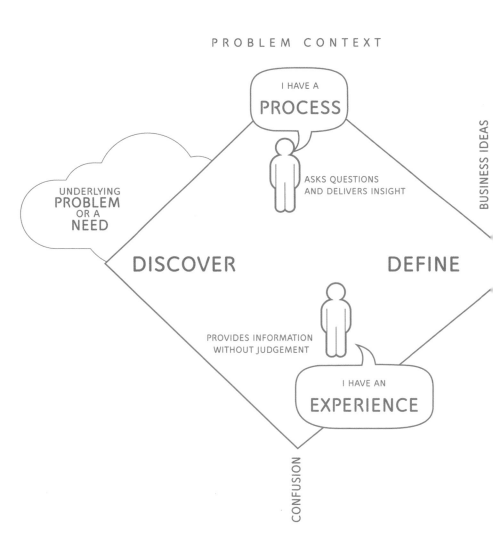

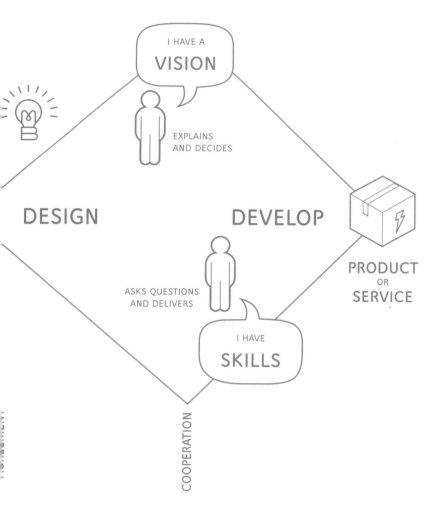

leader to make sense of the information and provide insight. In the execution phase later on, the roles might be reversed because the vision for the product may be provided by those that understand the technology, whereas the design specialist may provide only professional skill.

Just the beginning

This book is about service design – but really it is about only a very narrow piece of this discipline. Namely, this book is about the process of figuring out what customers actually think about your product or service and can help identify where you have problems. This book does not include every tool, every method, every means to design services.

If there are four D's in design – discover, define, develop and deliver – then this book is about just the first D: Discover. It explains how to learn to find information without expecting a concrete result. The rest will come later.

Changing the
organizational mindset

With many of our larger clients, the challenge is not in improving the service or process. Often, this could be done easily and quickly, if it weren't for the organization itself. Larger businesses have units, or silos, that work almost as independent companies, actively competing with other business units. Internal competition drives people, and motivation schemes are built around defeating internal metrics. Things "can't be done" because these changes would involve some other division, and that division would never agree to change, because it would influence their core product negatively. And so on, ad nauseum.

The largest challenge we face on a daily basis is not making processes easier and services better for the customer but rather convincing the organization that there is a better way of serving their customers. It is not easy to build the confidence of the organization to work in a different manner.

This becomes increasingly difficult with centralized businesses, where some core competencies are handled for the whole group from some other place. One of our clients is stuck with an antiquated cashier system, which due to the fact that the mother company is dominant on its market, is an urgent issue on our client's market but cannot be influenced. Furthermore, as markets move at different speeds, it is clearly noticeable that some technological solutions implemented as state-of-the-art 10-15 years ago are too expensive to scrap, but mainly useless in today's Bring-Your-Own-Device environment.

Whether the customer's perspective is addressed by outside consultants, or by an in-house team, the greatest challenge in the beginning will be to prove that the service design approach works. In order to apply it fully, a company must reconsider its organizational mindset, persuading employees of the benefits of service design beyond a shadow of a doubt.

In many industries, the requirement of proof is going to take too much time and effort to save the business. Banks with whom we've worked are in many cases seeing their business change completely. Organized into self-financing silos, with legacy technology systems that presume great interest, they are often the epitome of an inward facing business. Metrics are based on earnings per share, not customer satisfaction. Technological disruption, the growth of non-state-backed currencies, and general customer dissatisfaction can disrupt the whole industry much the same way that the post office, telcos, and broadcast TV have experienced.

The problem, ironically, is that the businesses facing the greatest turmoil are making the biggest profit presently. Banking is exactly there. Nokia was there, before the iPhone. Sony was there before the iPod. Kodak was there, before digital photography. Point-and-shoot camera makers are (maybe were) there before phone cameras became good enough for most people.

To design the future, the organization must first let go of the past. As people are naturally resistant to change, the work is mostly about changing the organization and only secondly, the customer experience.

Appendix

Tools

Here are short descriptions of tools for research, prototyping, testing, changing and finally implementing. There are many different methods for effective prototyping of service concepts. Below is an incomplete list that explains where and when to apply various techniques.

Research tools

Customer journey. The easiest and best way to understand where the value of the product or service is for the customer. Mapping the customer journey places the product or service into the context of a person's life, how it is acquired and discarded and clearly details the process that a person goes through to get the service and / or product and what is done to get rid of it.

Customer conversations. Lightly structured interviews with customers, based on a hypothesis created by analysis of the customer journey. Allows for validation / rejection of viewpoints and provides insight for actual customer motivation. Requires the interviewer to have a broad understanding of the project, in order to be able to interpret information and its relevance.

Customer observation. Because people are people, they may not be completely honest. People will say one thing and do another. Sometimes it is much more effective to observe behavior rather than understand it through an interview. Crowd mentality will affect how people act in situations, no matter what their individual impetus may be.

Contextual stakeholder interviews. The customer experience is often dependent on delivery by other stakeholders. The challenges facing other stakeholders in their work must be charted. Interviewing at the point of delivery can provide very good insight of what can be improved. The five "why's" – (asking 5 times why as a means of drilling down on reason why things are the way they are) – are effective in uncovering causes

Stakeholder observation. In some cases interviews with stakeholders must be complemented with silent observation. This can be because of the nature of the work or because there seems to be a discrepancy between what is said and what is observed. When observing, it is important not to influence those being observed.

In-depth research

A day in the life. A day-in-the-life is a diary method whereby participants detail how their day looks using pictures, video and notes. Smartphones are an incredible asset for this type of ethnographic research. This is especially useful in cases where empathy is difficult to achieve, or the target group is dispersed over a wide geographic area that cannot be conveniently researched. Note, however, that for this to be viable it requires a critical amount of participants.

Benchmarking of best cases. The customer journey details many touchpoints. Each touchpoint can be benchmarked to best-in-class samples, which can come both from within the same industry as well as from the world at large. Benchmarking in this manner broadens the perspective dramatically and really allows people within the organization to understand the customer's perspective.

Personas are richly detailed pictures of prototype customers. Workshop environments allow groups to focus the same service or product on clearly different people in order to understand the complexities of what the customer faces. Personas are an effective shortcut to understanding what needs to be researched in greater detail. However, they are not a substitute for talking to real people.

Workshops with customers. IImproving customer service with the customer has obvious benefits; the primary one being immediate validation of concepts. However, it is important to realize that co-creation with customers can also be misleading. Just because people say they will do something does not necessarily mean that they will do it in real life.

Scenario / prototype testing with customers. Having developed a detailed and illustrated hypothesis, it is possible to work with the target group to understand how clear or simple it is for them. This type of simple prototype validation (service prototypes tend to be pen and paper format) allows for quick iterations of the service concept and therefore saves a great deal of money in the long term, because the company will know not to invest in concepts which are incomprehensible to regular people.

Development

Agile / lean process management. Once concepts have been created and are ready for development, it makes sense to keep the process lean and simple. It should still involve all key stakeholders in the process and allow for quick iterations of services. These services can be tested live – in fact launched – with the ready understanding that they will also need to be improved immediately. However, as they are better than what they are replacing, this method allows for quick improvements. It is important therefore, that all stakeholders are involved and understand the big picture, because this way you can get away with a lack of detailed descriptions of procedure.

Service blueprinting. Service blueprinting draws out the whole service chain. It is used for validating ideas and concepts with different stakeholders and services as the birds-eye-view of the whole business. It maintains a strict customer perspective and as such must continuously be also tested and confirmed with customers.

About the author

Since 1992, J.Margus Klaar has been working in the advertising and marketing industry. Over the years he became disillusioned by his role in making average products better. He realized, that in the changing media and technology landscape it was no longer enough to just look good. Products and services had to be good, in order to earn their customers' loyalty.

In 2009, with three partners, he started the service design and branding consultancy Brand Manual. Since then, Brand Manual has been a pioneer of service design and helped improve a multitude of brands and companies from the inside out, to be better, not just look better.

He is 43 years old and lives in Stockholm, Sweden with his family.